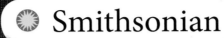 Smithsonian

THE NATIONAL MUSEUM OF
AMERICAN HISTORY

BY MEGAN COOLEY PETERSON

CAPSTONE PRESS
a capstone imprint

Smithsonian is published by Capstone Press,
1710 Roe Crest Drive, North Mankato, Minnesota 56003
www.mycapstone.com

Library of Congress Cataloging-in-Publication Data
Names: Peterson, Megan Cooley, author.
Title: The National Museum of American History / by Megan Cooley Peterson.
Description: North Mankato, Minnesota : Capstone Press, 2018.
I Series: Smithsonian field trips I Includes bibliographical references and index.
Identifiers: LCCN 2017011302I ISBN 9781515779766 (library binding) I ISBN 9781515779889 (pbk.)
I ISBN 9781515780069 (ebook pdf)
Subjects: LCSH: National Museum of American History (U.S.)—Juvenile literature.
Classification: LCC E169.1 .P4825 2018 I DDC 069.09753—dc23
LC record available at https://lccn.loc.gov/2017011302

Editorial Credits
Michelle Hasselius, editor; Sarah Bennett, designer; Kelli Lageson, media researcher;
Laura Manthe, production specialist

Our very special thanks to Kealy Gordon, Product Development Manager; and Ellen Nanney, Licensing Manager,
Smithsonian, for their assistance. Capstone would also like to thank the following at Smithsonian Enterprises:
Brigid Ferraro, Vice President, Education and Consumer Products; Carol LeBlanc, Senior Vice President, Education,
and Consumer Products; and Christopher A. Liedel, President.

Photo Credits
©2017 National Museum of American History, Kenneth E. Behring Center, Smithsonian: cover (all), 3, 4, 5, 6, 7
(top), 8 (top), 10 (top and bottom), 11 (top and bottom left), 12, 13 (top and bottom left), 14, 16 (top and bottom),
18 (bottom), 19 (top, bottom, and background), 20 (back, left, middle, and right), 21 (left and right), 22 (right),
23 (bottom), 24, 26 (bottom), 28; Alamy: VintageCorner, 22 (left); Granger, NYC - All rights reserved: 15 (bottom);
Library of Congress: 8 (bottom), 27 (bottom); National Archives and Records Administration: 17 (top left and
bottom), 23 (top left); Newscom: dpa/picture-alliance/DB Apple, 29 (top), History of Advertising Trust Heritage
Images, 11 (bottom right); Shutterstock: David M. Schrader, design element (throughout), Everett Historical, 7
(bottom), 9, 18 (top), 23 (middle right), 25 (top left and bottom), 27 (top), MaraZe, 13 (bottom right), 15 (top),
MitchR, 23 (top right), Morphart Creation, 25 (top right), Nor Gal, 29 (bottom), photo.ua, 5, Seashell World, 17
(top right), thatsmymop, 26 (top)

Printed in the United States of America.
010399F17

Table of Contents

Treasures at the Museum

Step into the past at the National Museum of American History in Washington, D.C. The Museum houses more than 3 million objects about American culture, military history, U.S. presidents, and scientific achievements. What treasures of American history will you discover?

—Fact—

The Museum first opened in January 1964. It was originally called the Museum of History and Technology.

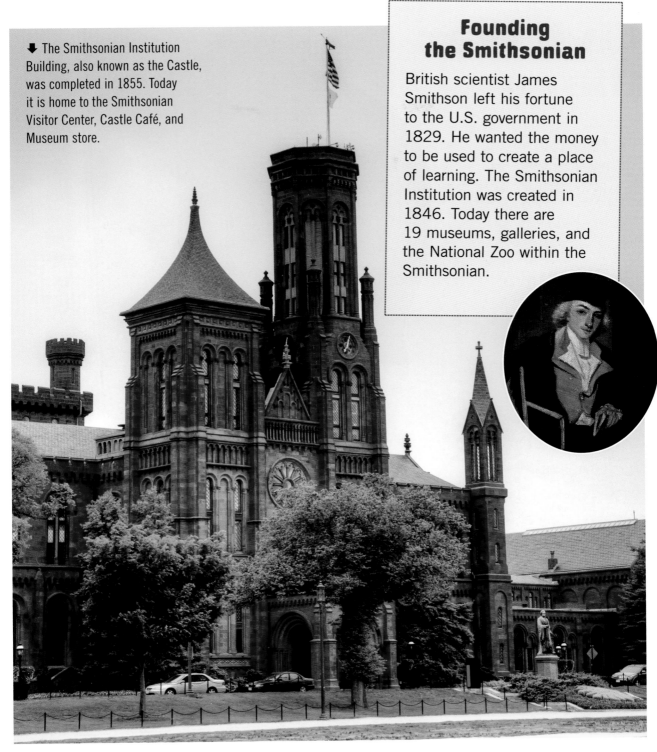

⬇ The Smithsonian Institution Building, also known as the Castle, was completed in 1855. Today it is home to the Smithsonian Visitor Center, Castle Café, and Museum store.

Founding the Smithsonian

British scientist James Smithson left his fortune to the U.S. government in 1829. He wanted the money to be used to create a place of learning. The Smithsonian Institution was created in 1846. Today there are 19 museums, galleries, and the National Zoo within the Smithsonian.

Civil War Diary

The Museum has a violin from the Civil War (1861–1865) in its collection. But this is no ordinary musical instrument.

On May 1, 1863, a Union solider named Solomon Conn bought a violin in Tennessee. But he didn't play it. Instead Conn carved the names of the battles he fought in and the places he visited onto his violin. When Conn died in 1926, the violin was passed down to his grandsons. They donated it to the Smithsonian in 1988.

Did You Know?

There are about 30 battles carved onto Conn's violin, including the Battle of Chickamauga in 1863 and the Battle of Kennesaw Mountain in 1864.

The Civil War and Slavery

The Civil War was the deadliest war in American history. More than 500,000 people died and 400,000 others were wounded. Slavery was a main cause of the Civil War. The northern states wanted to end slavery, but the southern states did not. The southern states seceded to form their own country, and the war began.

⬇ a photograph from 1865 of the 107th U.S. infantry band in Arlington, Virginia

—Fact—

Civil War soldiers often played musical instruments to pass the time. Bugles and drums were the most common instruments.

Calling the Future

— Fact —

Bell patented his telephone when he was 29. The patent protected his invention from being copied.

In the *American Stories* exhibit, visitors can see one of the first commercially available telephones. The large box telephone was invented by Alexander Graham Bell. On November 26, 1876, Bell demonstrated his invention. He called Salem, Massachusetts, from Boston, Massachusetts.

← Less than ten years after Bell demonstrated his telephone, a man works as a long-distance telephone operator at the American Telephone and Telegraph Company in Marietta, Georgia.

TIMELINE

1837

Samuel F. B. Morse makes the first practical telegraph machine.

1973

American inventor Martin Cooper makes the first phone call with a cell phone.

1993

IBM introduces Simon, the first smartphone.

2001

IBM introduces WatchPad, an early version of the smartwatch.

Medical Salves and Cure-alls

The National Museum of American History has more than 2,200 over-the-counter personal care products in its collection. In the 1800s these products were a big business in the United States. Companies made medicines and salves promising to cure everything from toothaches to cancer. Some cure-alls were even marketed for "man or beast." They claimed to cure people and their animals.

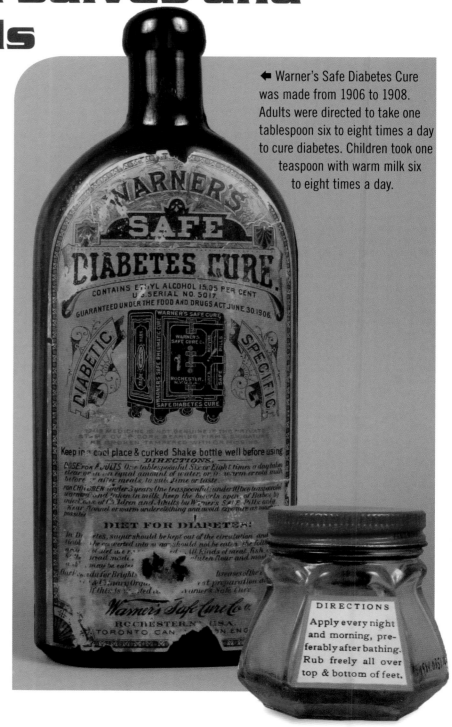

← Warner's Safe Diabetes Cure was made from 1906 to 1908. Adults were directed to take one tablespoon six to eight times a day to cure diabetes. Children took one teaspoon with warm milk six to eight times a day.

From 1898 to 1901, Dr. Hobbs Sparagus Kidney Pills promised to cure a number of ailments, including kidney and bladder problems, backaches, skin diseases, rashes, sleeplessness, nervousness, headaches, and dizziness.

False Advertising

Many cure-alls contained arsenic, lead, alcohol, and other drugs. The cure-alls provided temporary relief but no cures. Even when taken as recommended, many were harmful — even deadly. In 1906 Congress passed the Federal Food and Drugs Act. It forced companies to list the ingredients on their packages.

a container of Coolene Foot Creme from 1930

Did You Know?

In 1849 Mrs. Winslow's Soothing Syrup was introduced to consumers. The popular syrup for children promised to help relieve pain caused by teething. Although the product seemed to work, it contained a dangerous drug — morphine. Mrs. Winslow's Soothing Syrup was pulled from the market in the early 1900s.

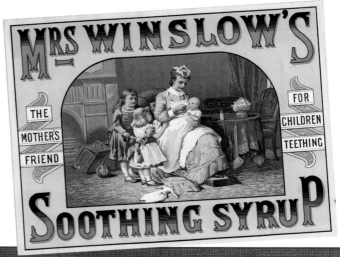

Ice Cream and the Refrigerator

In the 1800s people had to make ice cream at home. But only the wealthy could afford to. Ice cream lovers needed access to ice — lots of ice. In the winter they had to cut large blocks of ice from rivers and ponds and store them through the summer. Smaller ice cubes were chopped off the blocks. To make ice cream, cooks mixed together sugar, salt, eggs, and cream in a tin cylinder. Then they packed salt and ice around the tin. As they churned the cylinder, the ice "iced" the cream.

The home refrigerator changed all that. Home cooks didn't have to chip ice off a block to make this frozen treat. They mixed the ingredients and placed them in the freezer to firm up.

➡ an ice cream freezer from 1910 that had to be churned by hand

➡ George Doumar makes waffle cones for his ice cream stand with a special machine in 1920

⬇ "I Scream, You Scream, We All Scream for Ice Cream" was a popular song written in 1927. The song's title was also used as an advertising slogan for Eskimo Pies.

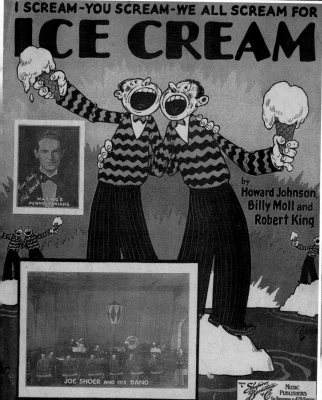

Did You Know?

In 1927 Alice Bradley published the cookbook, *Electric Refrigerator Recipes and Menus*. It included some of the first ice cream recipes for the freezer.

Greensboro Lunch Counter

On February 1, 1960, four African-American students entered a Woolworth's restaurant in Greensboro, North Carolina. During this time many places in the south were segregated. The students sat at a lunch counter reserved for white customers. Workers refused to serve them. When they were asked to leave, the students remained in their seats.

For the next six months, hundreds of civil rights activists, students, and church members protested the restaurant. Protests soon spread to 55 other cities. On July 25, 1960, Woolworth's desegregated its lunch counter. Black customers could now be served. In 1993 the restaurant closed. Four stools and an 8-foot (2.4-meter) section of the countertop were donated to the National Museum of American History.

↑ two members of the Greensboro Four, Joseph McNeil (left) and Franklin McCain (center), sit with other protesters at Woolworth's lunch counter on February 2, 1960

Clamshell Currency

The Great Depression of the 1930s was a hard time for many Americans. People lost their jobs. Banks failed. Money was hard to come by. In Pismo Beach, California, local businesses had a solution — clamshell currency. The city had an abundance of Pismo clams and shells. Each shell was numbered, signed, and assigned a dollar amount. People used the shells to buy items at participating businesses. When money became available again, people cashed in their clams for money.

➡ Pismo clamshells were worth between 25 cents and 20 dollars.

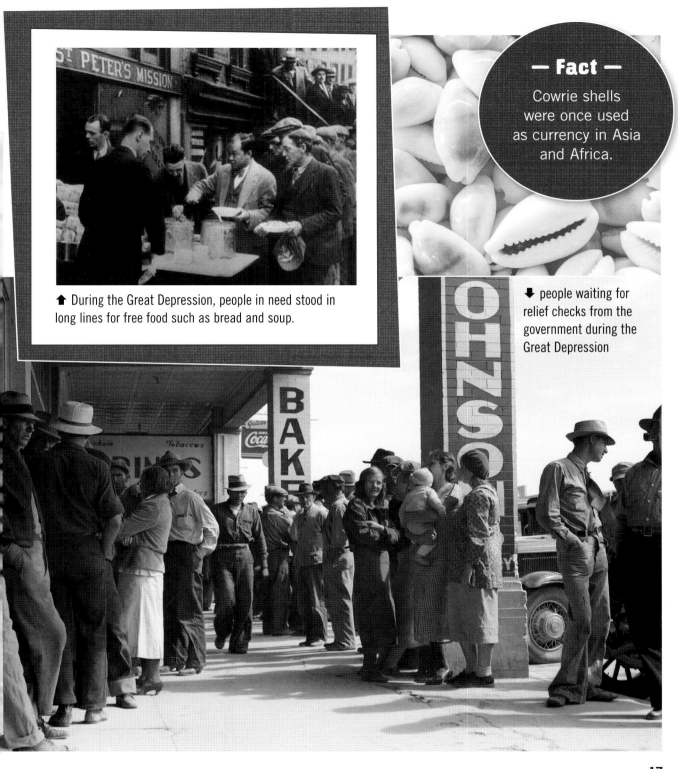

ST PETER'S MISSION

⬆ During the Great Depression, people in need stood in long lines for free food such as bread and soup.

⬇ people waiting for relief checks from the government during the Great Depression

Thomas Jefferson's Portable Desk

You probably sit at a desk every day at school. But did you know a desk was part of our nation's creation? In 1776 Thomas Jefferson wrote the Declaration of Independence on a portable desk. He designed the desk himself.

In 1825 Jefferson gave the desk to his granddaughter, Eleanora Randolph Coolidge, as a wedding present. The desk stayed in the Coolidge family until it was donated to the U.S. government in 1880.

— Fact —

Thomas Jefferson was the third president of the United States.

↑ The portable desk is about 10 inches (25 centimeters) long and 14 inches (35.5 cm) wide, a little larger than the first laptop computer.

"Politics as well as Religion has its superstitions. These, gaining strength with time, may, one day, give imaginary value to this relic, for its great association with the birth of the Great Charter of our Independence."

—the note Jefferson attached to the desk in 1825

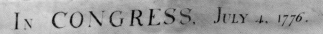

IN CONGRESS. JULY 4, 1776.

The unanimous Declaration of the thirteen united States of America.

◄ The Declaration of Independence was adopted on July 4, 1776. It established the United States of America as an independent nation.

Artificial Body Parts

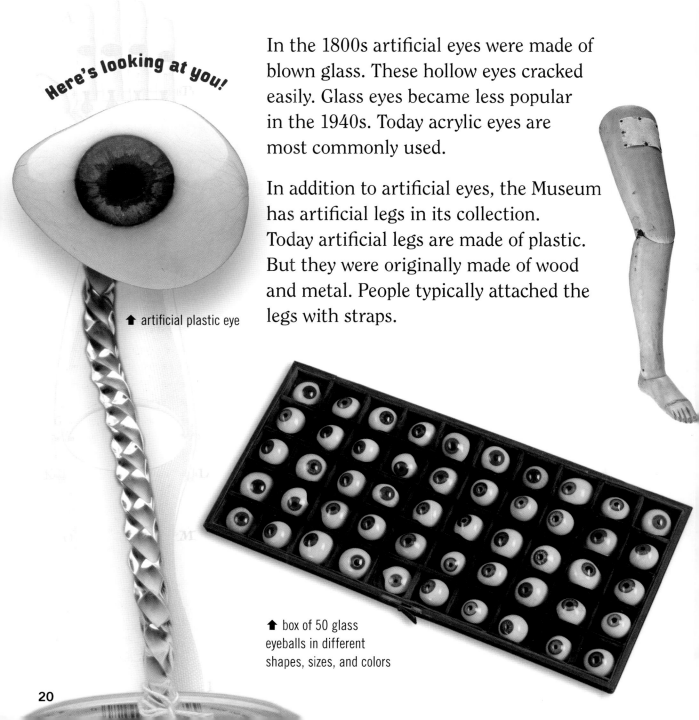

Here's looking at you!

In the 1800s artificial eyes were made of blown glass. These hollow eyes cracked easily. Glass eyes became less popular in the 1940s. Today acrylic eyes are most commonly used.

In addition to artificial eyes, the Museum has artificial legs in its collection. Today artificial legs are made of plastic. But they were originally made of wood and metal. People typically attached the legs with straps.

⬆ artificial plastic eye

⬆ box of 50 glass eyeballs in different shapes, sizes, and colors

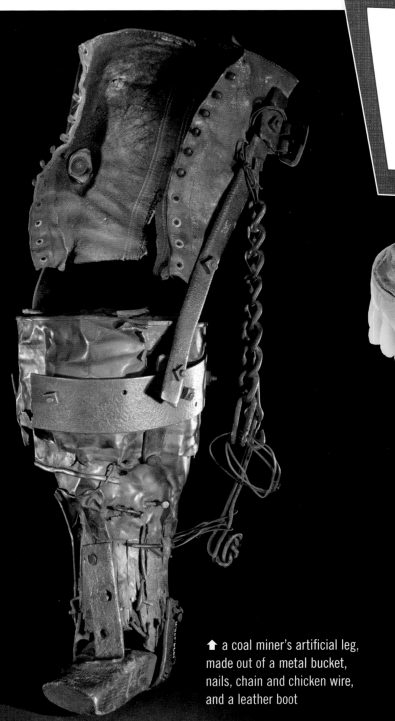

⬆ President George Washington is known for having false teeth. Many people believe they were made of wood, but his teeth were actually made out of ivory.

⬆ a coal miner's artificial leg, made out of a metal bucket, nails, chain and chicken wire, and a leather boot

Cher Ami

During World War I
(1914–1918), the U.S.
military used pigeons to
carry important messages
to and from the battlefields.
A carrier pigeon named
Cher Ami was one of 600
birds used by the U.S. Army
Signal Corps during the
war. Cher Ami delivered
12 messages.

⬇ The French Army awarded Cher Ami one of its highest honors, the French Croix de Guerre with Palm, for the pigeon's heroic service.

Did You Know?

The American Red Star Animal
Relief was created in 1916.
It helped animals that were
wounded in the war.

Help him to help U.S.!

Help the
Horse to
Save the
Soldier

THE AMERICAN RED STAR ANIMAL RELIEF
National Headquarters. Albany. N.Y.

↑ an American solider attaches a message to a Signal Corps carrier pigeon during World War I

On its last mission, Cher Ami was wounded. But the bird was able to deliver the message and helped save the lives of 194 soldiers. When the carrier pigeon died in 1919, it was donated to the Museum. Cher Ami is now part of the *Price of Freedom: Americans at War* exhibit.

Sluggish Heroes

Slugs also helped save the lives of U.S. soldiers during World War I. They were used to detect deadly mustard gas. The slugs curled up near the gas. When soldiers saw this, they knew to put on their gas masks.

⬇ A Staffordshire terrier mix named Stubby was the first dog given a rank in the United States Armed Forces. He served in 17 battles during World War I. Stubby is also part of the *Price of Freedom: Americans at War* exhibit at the Smithsonian.

Thomas Edison's Light Bulb

QUICK! Turn on the light!

On New Year's Eve 1879, Thomas Edison had a special surprise in store for the public. He lit up his street in Menlo Park, New Jersey, with light bulbs. It was the first public display of electric light bulbs. One of Edison's light bulbs is in the Museum's *American Enterprise* exhibit.

➡ Edison received the patent for his electric light bulb on January 27, 1880.

Did You Know?

Edison didn't invent the light bulb, but he improved it. Other bulbs burned for only a few seconds. Edison's bulbs burned for more than 40 hours.

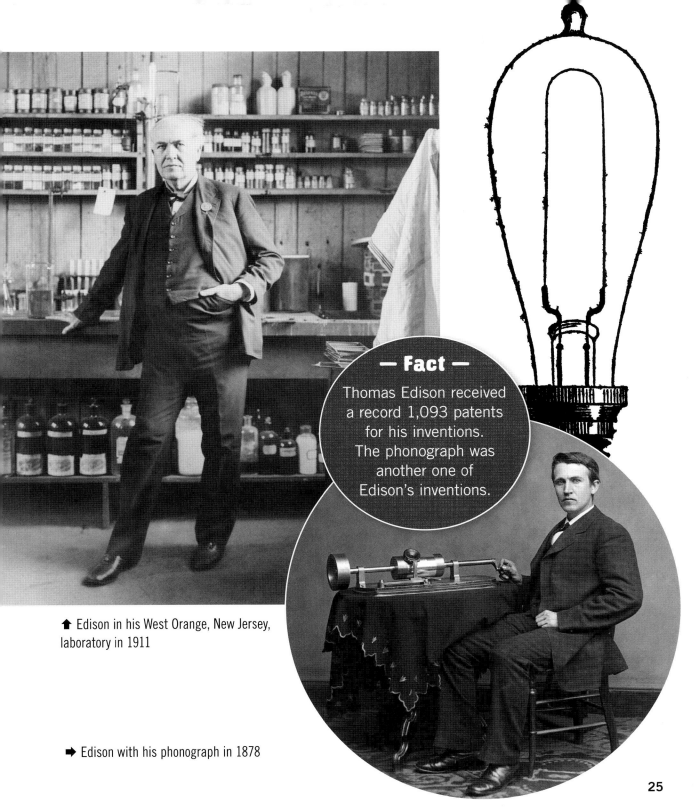

⬆ Edison in his West Orange, New Jersey, laboratory in 1911

➡ Edison with his phonograph in 1878

Presidential Top Hat

⬆ Lincoln kept important papers in the lining of his top hat.

On April 14, 1865, President Abraham Lincoln wore his signature top hat to Ford's Theatre. While Lincoln was enjoying a play, John Wilkes Booth shot him. Lincoln died from his injuries. The War Department kept Lincoln's hat. It was given to the Smithsonian in 1867.

⬇ the front of Ford's Theatre after President Lincoln was assassinated

⬇ The train that carried Lincoln's body was called The Lincoln Special. Lincoln's portrait was attached to the front of the train's engine.

Did You Know?

A train transported Lincoln's body to Illinois. It stopped in 180 cities along the way. At each stop people could view the president in his coffin.

— Fact —

John Wilkes Booth was a famous actor. Abraham Lincoln was a fan.

Apple II Computer

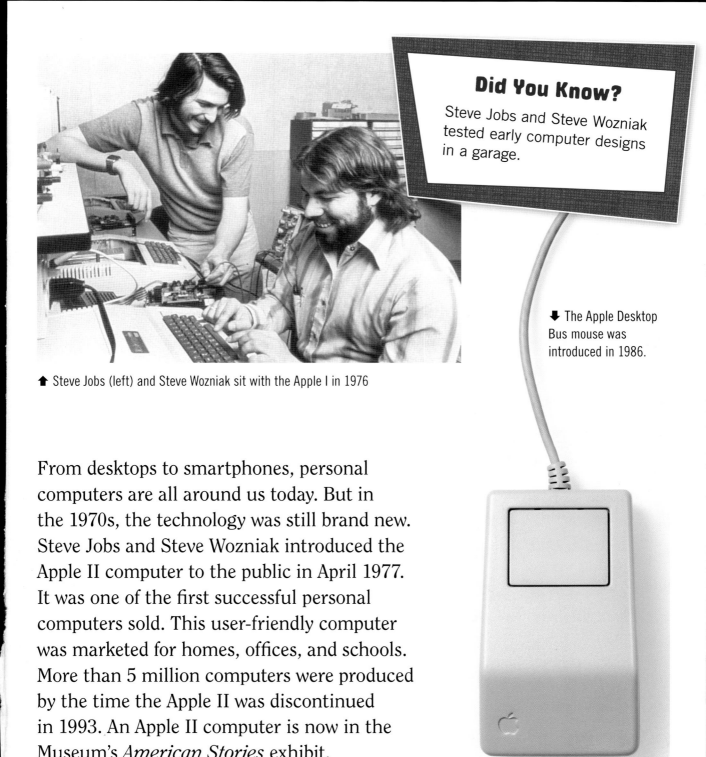

↑ Steve Jobs (left) and Steve Wozniak sit with the Apple I in 1976

⬇ The Apple Desktop Bus mouse was introduced in 1986.

From desktops to smartphones, personal computers are all around us today. But in the 1970s, the technology was still brand new. Steve Jobs and Steve Wozniak introduced the Apple II computer to the public in April 1977. It was one of the first successful personal computers sold. This user-friendly computer was marketed for homes, offices, and schools. More than 5 million computers were produced by the time the Apple II was discontinued in 1993. An Apple II computer is now in the Museum's *American Stories* exhibit.

Glossary

acrylic (uh-KRIH-lik)—a chemical substance used to make fibers and paints

arsenic (AR-suh-nik)—a chemical element that usually appears as a gray-white powder and is poisonous if swallowed

bugle (BYOO-guhl)—a musical instrument shaped like a trumpet without keys

culture (KUHL-chur)—a group of people's beliefs, customs, and way of life

currency (KUR-uhn-see)—the form of money used in a country

donate (DOH-nate)—to give something as a gift

patent (PAT-uhnt)—a legal document giving the inventor of an item sole rights to manufacture or sell the item

phonograph (FOH-nuh-graf)—a machine that picks up and reproduces the sounds that have been recorded in the grooves of a record

salve (SAV)—an ointment or a cream that relieves pain and helps heal wounds, burns, or sores

secede (si-SEED)—to formally withdraw from a group or an organization, often to form another organization

segregate (SEG-ruh-gate)—to separate or keep people or things apart from the main group

telegraph (TEL-uh-graf)—a device or system for sending messages over long distances; the telegraph used a code of electrical signals sent by wire or radio

Union (YOON-yuhn)—the northern states that fought against the southern states in the Civil War